WEST CHICAGO P
3 6653 00048 9553
P9-CFI-858

The *Let's-Read-and-Find-Out Science Book* series was originated by Dr. Franklyn M. Branley, Astronomer Emeritus and former Chairman of the American Museum–Hayden Planetarium, and was formerly co-edited by him and Dr. Roma Gans, Professor Emeritus of Childhood Education, Teachers College, Columbia University. For a complete catalog of Let's-Read-and-Find-Out Science Books, write to HarperCollins Children's Books, 10 East 53rd Street, New York, NY 10022.

 Printed in the United States of America. For information address HarperCollins Children's Books, a division of HarperCollins Publishers, 10 East 53rd Street, New York, NY 10022.
1 2 3 4 5 6 7 8 9 10
Revised Edition

Library of Congress Cataloging-in-Publication Data
Hawes, Judy.
Fireflies in the night / by Judy Hawes ; illustrated by Ellen Alexander. — Rev. ed.
p. cm. — (Let's-read-and-find-out science book)
Summary: Describes how fireflies make their light, tells how to catch and handle them, and notes several interesting uses for firefly light.
ISBN 0-06-022484-3.—ISBN 0-06-022485-1 (lib. bdg.)
1. Fireflies—Juvenile literature. [1. Fireflies.]
I. Alexander, Ellen, ill. II. Title. III. Series.
QL596.L28H38 1991 90-1587
595.76'44—dc20 CIP
AC

The illustrations were done in pastels on Rives smooth watercolor paper.

This Is a Let's-Read-and-Find-Out Science Book®

Revised Edition

FIREFLIES IN THE NIGHT

by Judy Hawes

illustrated by Ellen Alexander

HarperCollinsPublishers

I like fireflies. When I visit my grandfather in the summertime, we sit outdoors after supper and watch them.

FIREFLIES IN THE NIGHT

Grandmother likes to watch fireflies too. She calls them lightning bugs. They look like little dancing stars. They are really beetles, Grandfather says.

All beetles have two sets of wings and so do fireflies. When they rest, they fold their hard front wings on top of their soft back wings.

Young fireflies do not have wings at all. For their first year or two they live in the ground, just like young beetles. When their wings grow, they live above ground in trees or bushes.

Grandfather gave me a glass jar to use on firefly hunts. We punched holes in the lid.

Fireflies are easy to catch. Soon my jar is lighted up like a lantern.

After every firefly hunt, Grandfather has something new to tell me. One time he showed me how to make my firefly lantern brighter. (He promised it would not hurt my fireflies.) Just hold the jar upright in a bowl of warm water.

He knew it would work because fireflies always shine brighter in warm weather. If you dip the jar in cold water, the firefly lights will fade.

People in hot countries make good use of firefly light. In the Caribbean, and in some parts of South America, people sometimes wear net bags full of fireflies tied to their wrists or ankles. These homemade flashlights help them find their way along the dark jungle paths.

Grandfather let me try this in the cornfield because we have no jungle.

In Japan, the gardens are lighted at night by firefly lanterns. That must be nice!

Grandfather also told me about a doctor in Cuba who, many years ago, once used a firefly lamp in his operating room. His other lights had gone out!

Fireflies make *cold* light. Candles make hot light. If I put one tiny birthday candle in a jar, the jar gets too hot to hold. My firefly lantern never gets warm.

I asked my grandfather, "How can fireflies make cold light?" He told me that fireflies have special chemicals inside them. When fireflies take in air, the air mixes with these chemicals. Flash!—the mixture makes light *without heat*.

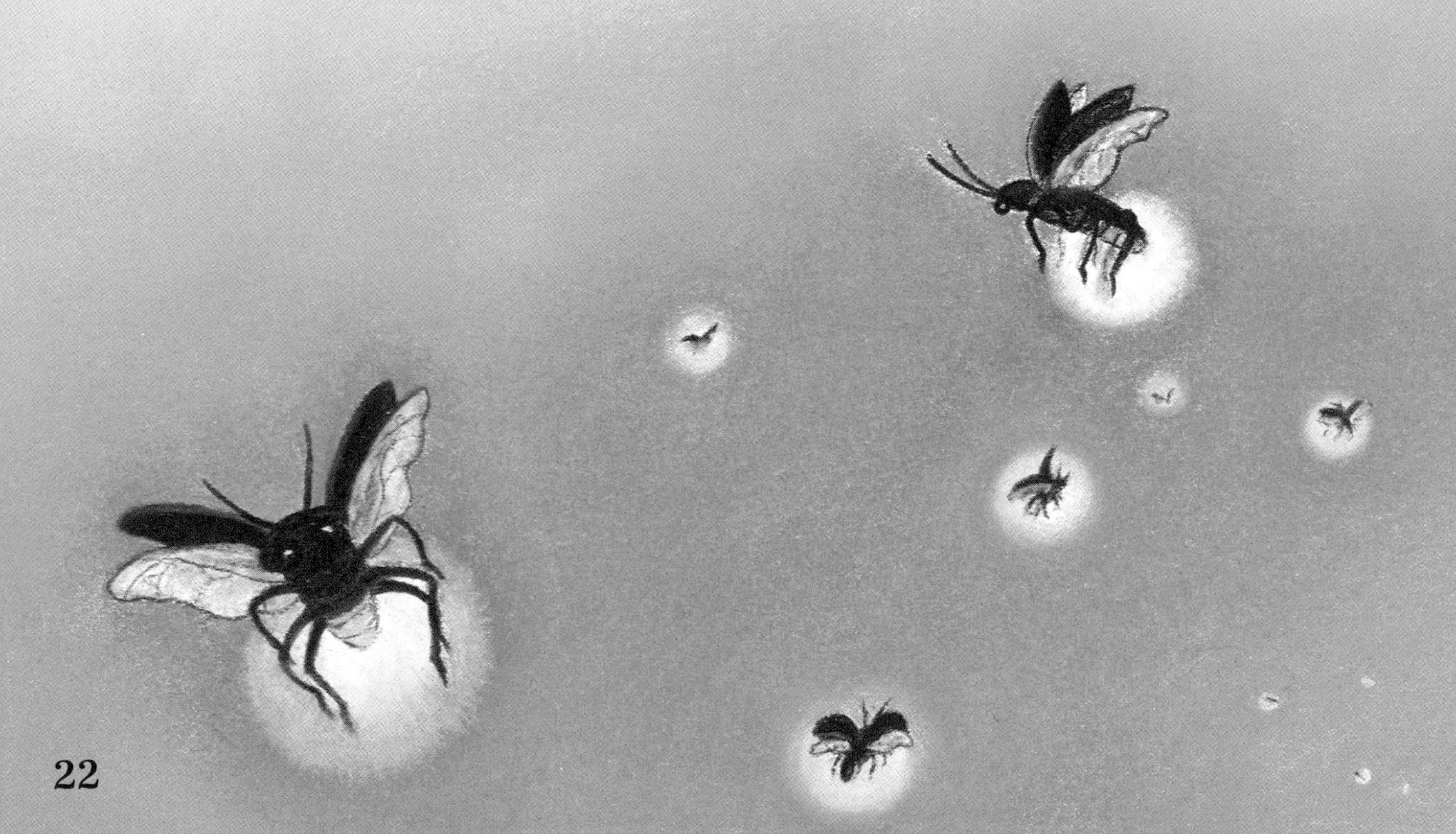

Small holes on the side of the firefly let air in. The special chemicals mix with air in the underpart of the firefly. These chemicals plus air equal cold light.

Fireflies have special ways to flash their lights which they repeat over and over. Each kind signals in a different pattern of flashes and pauses. As he flies around, a male firefly may make a signal like this: 3 or 4 or 5 quick flashes. Wait for six seconds. Repeat.

A female firefly stays in the grass and gives her own kind of answering signal, probably like this: 1, 2, or 3 quick flashes. Wait for two seconds. Repeat. That's how fireflies find their mates.

Grandfather says if I sit quietly in the grass and flash a small flashlight on and off every two seconds, the fireflies may be fooled and come to *me*! I am going to try that tomorrow night.

Tonight I am taking my firefly lantern to my secret hideaway. Under the bedcovers my lantern makes a cozy light. Just for me!

My grandmother will come soon to say goodnight.

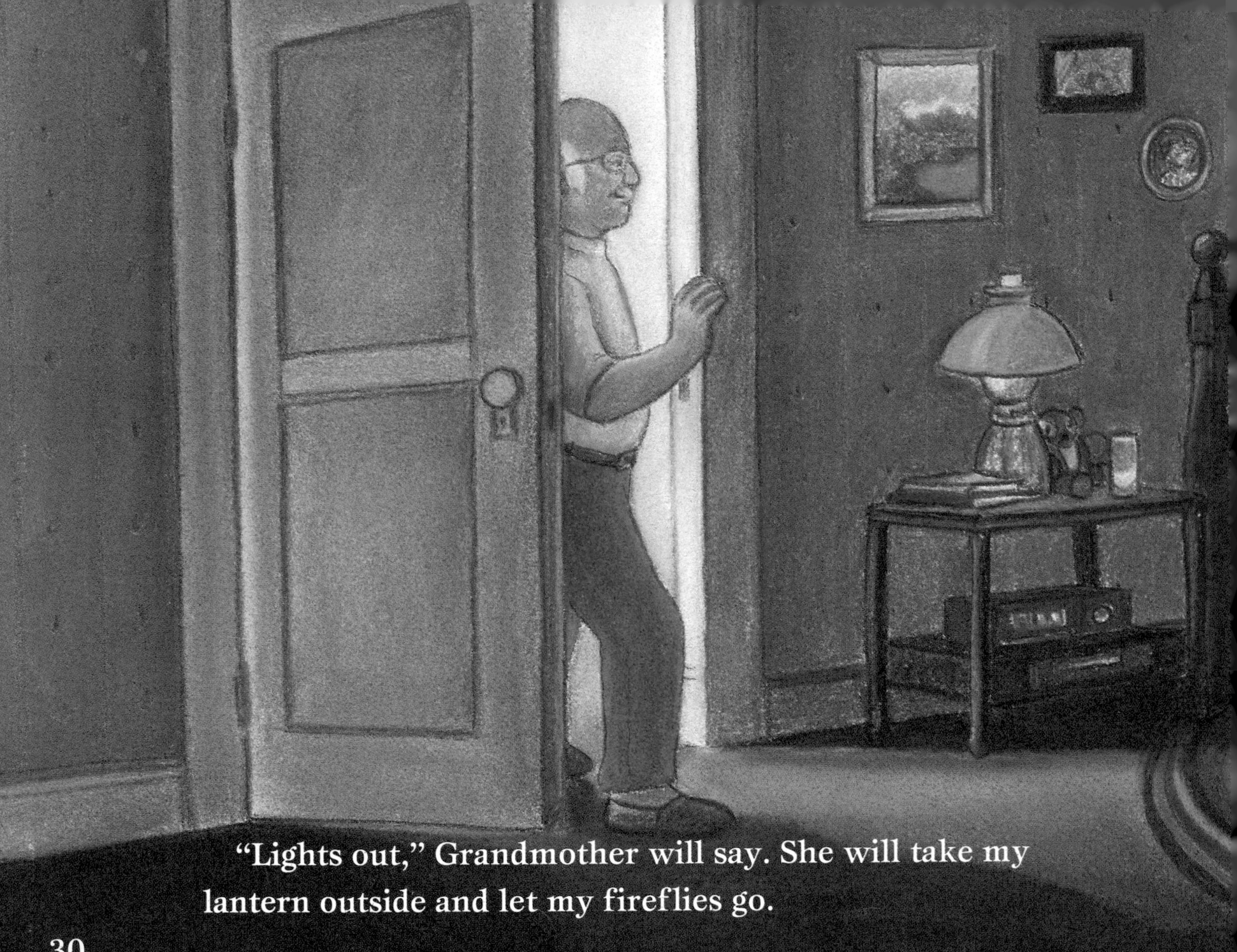

"Lights out," Grandmother will say. She will take my lantern outside and let my fireflies go.

I'll catch some more tomorrow night.